50

CHRISTMAS MINIATURES

A Heartwarming Coloring Book with 50 Cheerful Illustrations of Cute Christmas Baby Animals, Small Quirky Houses, Festive Winter Scenes, and Much More

Kameliya Angelkova

BOOK DETAILS:

Cute! Merry! Festive!

50 funny, curious, and enjoyable hand-drawn designs to color the whole winter season!

50 entertaining Christmas and winter drawings, as well as bunch of small scenes, featuring various cute animals, festive decorations, winter plants, fancy doors, houses, diminutive lanterns, and even more to keep you pleased and relaxed till spring!

Easy, complete line art: The illustrations in this book need very little time to be fully colored. That's why they are called "miniatures". Among them you will find some easier and some more detailed ones to fit to your needs.

Separately-printed (white background) drawings: Every illustration is printed alone on a white, non-perforated paper (the right pages).

A letter sized, large printed book of: 8.5 inches x 11.0 inches (22 x 28 cm) dimensions.

Glossy, festive-themed cover image.

Ideal for any high-quality art mediums, such as markers, crayons, or softer pencils. Not recommended for gel pens, watercolors, or any too wet mediums. In any case, do not forget to put a sheet of paper right below the image you are coloring, to eliminate the bleeding on the next design.

This Christmas book might be a great choice for a winter, or festive gift, a pretty collectible for your book shelfs, or for your videos!

NO numerations, gray, black, or grayscale spaces.

NO spiral bounds or perforations.

NO illustrations are doubled.

NON of the lines are too wide or too thin.

THIS BOOK
BELONGS TO:

_____

_____

MORE MINIATURES COLORING BOOKS:

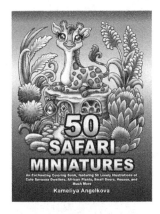  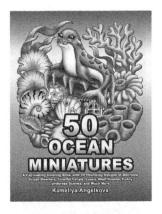 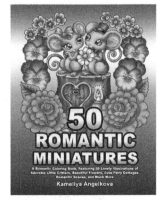

SEASONAL MINIATURES COLORING BOOKS:

   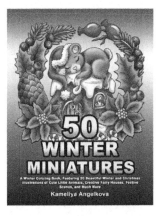

BLACK BACKGROUND MINIATURES:

SEASONAL MANDALA COLORING BOOKS:

DREAM-CATCHERS :

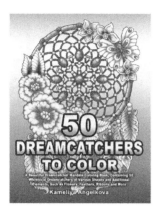

MANDALAS ON BLACK BACKGROUND :

SPIRAL-SWIRLY MANDALAS:

EASY COLORING BOOKS:

INTRICATE MANDALAS:

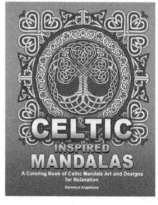

BIG MANDALA COLORING BOOKS:

FANTASY ART COLORING BOOKS:

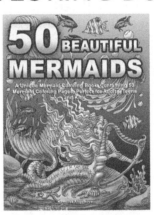

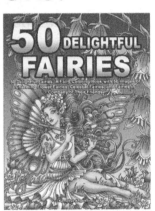

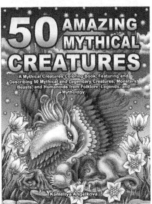

ABOUT THE AUTHOR OF THE BOOK

Kameliya Angelkova is a European author and illustrator of various adult coloring books (mandala and fantasy images). She works with desire for improvement, much imagination, eagerness, and true love for art. The artist tries to make genuine, quirky, adorable, and delightful designs. So, if you enjoy her books, don't hesitate to rate them and post your positive reviews on Amazon. Follow the author and check her author's page for new releases (see below)!

~~~~

Find all books and updates on the official Amazon page of the author:

www.amazon.com/author/kameliyaangelkova

For flip through videos, colored pages and book previews visit:

VIDEO FLIPS: youtube.com/kameliyaangelkova

COLORED PAGES: instagram.com/coloring.art.relax

pinterest.com/kameliyaangelkova

OFFICIAL WEBSITE: www.quotestipsbooks.wordpress.com

Made in the USA
Las Vegas, NV
17 May 2022

49019415R00063